Is,
The Color
Of
Mississippi
Mud

&

Lou
  Next
Door

Two Vignettes of Poetry
  by
Charles Curtis Blackwell

Editors: Vincent Kobelt
           James L. Martin

Is, the Color Of Mississippi Mud
by
Charles Curtis Blackwell

Cover Design:
Charles Curtis Blackwell

Published by lulu.com
Copyright 2000 & 2008

Copies can be acquired at lulu.com
Is, the Color of Mississippi Mud &
Lou Next Door
Content ID: 1077073

Table of Contents

Introduction

Is, The Color Of Mississippi Mud is a long narrative poem in two sections whose structure lies somewhere between an epic variant and an allegory. At first glance, it appears to be an epic poem, but there is no individual, heroic central figure that one usually finds in most epics. Instead, the central figure is a collectivity of southern black folk who are more tragic than heroic, unless "heroism" can be found and measured by the degree to which they are determined to survive within a harsh, unjust, unrelenting racist society.

The setting does not cover great nations as does a regular epic. Instead, Blackwell has as his setting the rural areas and small towns of Mississippi. Mississippi, thus becomes a symbol for the entire American South and by extension, and to a great extent, a metaphor for the black culture that was
spawned there in the southern plantations and cotton fields, buttressed by the vagaries of prejudice and discrimination.

The action in Blackwell's epic consists of the extraordinary human courage of black people who had the courage to endure lynching:

    the moss hung from the trees
    the neighbors hung from the trees

The Ku Klux Klan:

    Klansman grown weary
    in their plight
    their wives washing laundry
    and cleaning sheets
    attending meetings
    and January white sheet sales…

Poverty:

    sorry is
    a sorry word
    the culture of poverty
    is a sorry place

Slavery:

    and African tribesmen
    gather
    strangers to one another
    standing at attention

and standing in chains
listening and waiting for...

The style employed in an epic poem is supposed to be "sustained
elevation and grand simplicity." Instead,
Blackwell's poetic style is highly complex. It seems to have
evolved from his attempt to give simultaneous expression to the
flow of images, sensations, perceptions, words, ideas, illogical
associations (and some things that cannot be articulated). This is
usually done in a staccato, cacophonous, improvisatory manner,
not unlike jazz riffs.

Is, The Color of Mississippi Mud episodically comments on
Race relations in America as seen from the perspective of southern
black folks with telling poignancy and imagery (a pregnant rat
tries to catch boat up stream by entering a bale of cotton). The
recurring incidents among the collective folk of miscarried justice;
hopelessness bred from superstition, fear, and illiteracy; the
longing for a better life are all bound together by the blood-red
Mississippi mud.

Allan M. Gordon, Ph.D.

Beginning Note

Mrs. Dolly Fong caught my arm with a strong grip as I was about to head out the door. She had read me like a book. During high-school English, a white student referred to me with a racial slur and then spoke another racial remark to Mrs. Fong. Now I knew I could get him and I was determined to beat the life out of him even if his friends jumped in. It was the same situation every day, racial insults, being kicked, pushed against lockers, and this time I decided I would change it by fighting it my way.

Mrs. Fong wouldn't let go of my arm. She called my name with a gripping sound that came from deep within. "Charles! You can't fight bigotry with violence. You must study and learn and become educated. That's how you fight prejudice and bigotry."

When someone really cares for another we feel it. Like God at work, she wouldn't let go of my arm. And as she spoke those words she shook me. For, though I thought I was just another student, she was concerned about me as an African-American headed for the hospital or jail.

I was about weep, had a sullen face, but I wanted to smile and act like it didn't affect me.

I'm grateful I listened.

Three years at the California high school and on that one day I received the real tools of education from Mrs. Fong.

Is, The Color of Mississippi Mud

It looks like
Someone had clay
And one eyedropper
And held high
Let drops of blood fall
To become
This red dusty dirt
You know
What was a slave
And a bigger
Once a freed man
Would-be neighbor
Referred to as a "nigger"
Was brutally killed
Too weak
This mud
It's a strange color
Here in Mississippi
This red dusty dirt

As if souls
bearing spirits
had been
      tarnished
in this red mud
it's a strange color
carrying sounds and pictures of slaves
up and down
ruts in the road
it's a strange color
to live
to suffer
or haunt
weeks ago
in years past
thrashing
his insides
outsides
they killed and they killed
a being
the hour of mud
tarnished streets and
a swan-like figure held high
and slaves can be seen
in this red dusty dirt
this mud is a strange color
carrying
scars of poverty

tears of despair
      standing in the
           ditches
this mud that
migrated
from here to every slave and
former slaves remaining
children's uprising
encompassed by a revolt
that never existed

They come as thieves in the night
Corinth
past ages
they come violent
they come bringing violence
Corinth
still moist in the night
they come
with evil and no eyes
bearing
no faces
their hands and
white sheets
can be seen even
with the sweat
for they come
to spread fear

for they come to kill
my mother
not knowing that her spirit
after death
will rise at
12:00 o'clock
always wanting to be free
but returning in a ghost-like way
for revenge

A mockingbird plays a
sporadic bundle of notes
to itself
while others unnoticing
hear and listen
as though nothing has
ever happened
ignorance
a mockingbird sighs
as violence continues
past Corinth
no passage from
                violence
how many times?
how many roads?
how many ruts?
and how many lives lived?
again
but how many bridges

must be crossed
in flight
sermons preached
with sweat as words
remaining on a dusty
highway 15
along with chains
preacher man
preacher man
when will the land
deliver me
when will the land
deliver me
cries an old woman
in sorrow, in sadness
with her hands
lifted up in a
Corinth Negro Baptist church
wanting to be free

No use pretending that this place
doesn't exist
the reality of the ghost
stands before us
face to face
bearing arms
we empty our smiles
in fear of not standing

until the very love
that was placed here at
birth is choked
out
release me
cries Corinth
release me
deliver me
oh Lawd
cries Corinth
as she bears
a child

into a world of
misery
tears
red clay dirt
and red mud

Night riders in the mist
babies crying
heat rising from the past day's sun
night riders in the mist
passing and caring
they roam and scrounge
leaving babies to cry
all the roads
night riders know

never worry
just sleep in peace on a
pea hull mattress
right night riders
move in the mist
the rain has lifted
night riders have passed
through Corinth
leaving death
stuck on tar and feathers
their friendship
so moving, touching
the rain has lifted
the mud has settled
and a small Negro child
walks barefoot
in the same direction
as the mud scurries
through the ditch
which he comes out of toting a pail of water
from a neighbor's well and
passing death on the
back side of an oak tree
left by the night riders in the mist

Maggie's farm
upstream
up the river

and a mule named Doc
upstream and up the river
and up yours
WELCOME TO THE MASON DIXON LINE

So long yonder way
on past Maggie's farm
chains
blending and bending
rock to sand
sand to ashes
crushing
pounding out the sound
of
chains
chain gangs cussing
chains crossing
Maggie's farm
a pregnant mule
in the barn
chains
running
roads
Parchman's farm
spelling
chains
16 rabbits
one coon dog
and an unplowed field of cotton

That refuses to be picked

The full moon passed last night
and so did Sister Mattie Jones
a faithful member

from Mount Ples
and no light shines for
hours
or ours to be
in passing
come Saturday
come mourners
come weeping
come sadness of speech
rut
that's the way of
living and that's the
way of life
for as we have known it
and for as we are to go
ashes to ashes
and red clay dirt
to red clay dirt
faithful member
from Mount Ples
and no light shines for
hours
or ours to be
in passing
come Saturday
come mourners
come weeping
come sadness of speech

ruts in the road
that's the way of
living and that's the
way of life
for as we have known it
and for as we are to go
ashes to ashes
and red clay dirt
to red clay dirt

Crows gather
each other
notwithstanding
their speech or manners
church members gather
flocking to each other
cornfields spun
down trodden to the fall
after rows upon rows
become remains splattered by the rain
thoughts of rage
stacked high
cornfields spun
mostly by the rain
a solemn face
cries a distant name
Lovester
Lovester
and the memories of cornfields

change
splattered by the rain
hands that once plowed
this field of pebbles
grip the edge of rain soaked
caskets
and an inside soul
searches
what beat and wrought
such a simple form of love
only in times of missing
can memories
come face to face
and so placid
and shower of the pain
raindrops
will build forever
the funeral in the rain
the cornfields and the pain
a passing crow
late at night that
etches out the mystery
of a name
Lovester
Lovester
fields of wrought
Lovester
Lovester

Gravediggers
return
neighbors to each other
money changers
gather
customers to one another
dirt will pile
and piles of dirt
wither away the time
and as to undermine
gravediggers
will heap piles on top of
piles
dry humid air turns
moist against a rusty
old shovel that can uproot
the thought of heading
upstream
of the Rock Island Line
but twice before we were told
to listen to the sound of
gravediggers
as they eat and plant
berries
as grave
voices spread fears
scattered by

the burst
of berries
rhythm of pickers
and piles of red clay dirt
become memories
of berries
and graves
use is useless
and repetition kills the soul
chains and picks
one day howling and pounding
the very depths of this
hole will be calling
home
      home

Red clay dirt
and angry mud
pitched in red
and scattered in the forms
of berries and graves
gravediggers
calling
home
      home
and hoping for
the river in crossing
lead me
upstream

oh baby
don't be so mean
raise my hand
in a Schuck town Baptist Church
and praise
and praise
and hope
for upstream
oh baby don't be so mean
for the mud has brought me here
and gravediggers tell me
where I'm going
and it's all before
I live

Rhythm and the rhyme
and the rhyme of the rhythm
seed-spitting contest
the inside strict
3-day old cow mess
in which ankles are healed
and heals are made whole
the rhythm and thyme
green stripes of a watermelon rind
inside the rhythm and the
rhyme of the rind
pound
A
pounding B flat

pound A, B flat, A, A
complications
rhythm
pound
rhythm
pounding
heartbeats
drums
rhythm
drum beats
thrash
rhythm
pounding beats
a hollow log
down home
distant sound
inside a hollow log
distance of the F flat
rhythm
rhythm
pound
rhythm
lonesome Mississippi
turned warm
by Arcelia's affection
speaking of
sad to be with you
knowing where you go and when you've gone

rhythm of the night
warm is the sweat
warm is the night
thrust hard
rhythm comes from inside
never ending
ride the tiny pebbles of
sweat from arm pits
rhythm and lips
and rhythm
and everywhere is the
fine red dusty dirt
even here with the
soft brown skin
lips
and soft is the mushiness thereof
mixed with the
rhythm
and the move of the moans
rhythm
and more pounding beats
until desperation
becomes a gasp of breath rhythm
more rhythm
pound
rhythm
pound
pound hump thrust

rhythm
rhythm groan

Melodies and beats
and notes there of
Dogan, Zulu, and
tribes before
African village
call out my name
flowers bloom
and drums pound
heart beats
barefoot in the mud
as tribesman carry
elephant tusks
to the boats
for crossing
tribesman like their crossing
gravediggers
plowing their feet
pounding barefoot in the mud
upstream through the River Nile
upstream through the night
none lasting
and tribesmen seen
still through the night
an abrupt move
bearing new children

into slavery
and each new slave was
borne
from Africa
and what the fuck
and what's the mother fuckin
industrialization up too
only to snuff you
only to snuff you
cries a white poor man
crippled from the
Elizabethan poor law
even though his eyes were
blue
his words were true
to snuff you
hurry home
come slavery
hurry home
come slavery
for bare-trodden souls
have fooled
and capitalism has won
and African tribesmen
gather
strangers to one another
standing at attention
and standing in chains

listening and waiting for
rhythms of sorrow unspoken

Winter came early this October, just after
the peas had been picked and picked over.

The cold wind from the north, mixed with
the mid-October rain, 'Caused nearby neighbors to
burn firewood and bust logs in preparation for a
long hard winter in America and in Mississippi.

Verreil sat looking out the window,
gazing as usual into the distant past dwindling
on the three husbands she buried, and loves of
her life, and loves she had lost.

But the winter would be cold and nearer
the reality of all approached slowly as she moves
her hand upwards carrying a drink of water to her
lips that her daughter drew from the well.

The right side of her body paralyzed from
four (4) strokes, her weight loss, and not saying
much these days, just gazing out the window
into a distant past.

Last night her daughter read the Bible to
her but little change it brought, for Verreil read
the Bible many times before and to her daughter
too.

Her daughter, Elcee, carrying a cross and
a heavy load, realizing we all have a cross to
bear and both she and Verreil stand in a pathway
in life waiting on death to come. A few pebbles

of rain on the window and grazed the outside
screen, rusted by last year's rain and the year
before while Verreil moved her eyes about
the windowpane, searching the raindrops for a
sigh of relief.

Johannah baby
you could have gone
anywhere
to lie and wait
or perhaps
to steal away
to me
or to Jesus
but Johannah
Johannah
what must I do
and what can I do
you've gone
and I am feelin
              so blue
Johannah
read my tears and
blue is the sky
and sweet were the years
no one loved
loved you better than I
a pond can go asunder

a thousand times
just by throwing
one rock into the middle
of an hour of the pond
one pond
a thousand times
pecans come back together again
Johannah baby
you didn't have to leave me
like this
in tears
one pond inside my soul
never to come back again
Johannah
Johannah baby
dry these tears
send Jesus
or tell him to
send me somebody to love
another
Johannah
to dry these tears
Johannah
Johannah
you didn't have to love me

We could have turned back
come tomorrow
and now I see today

the autumn leaves
sing close
to the nearby pines
Klansmen grow weary
their sheets clean
bearing no blood stains
lonesome long lost rodent
or parasite
in search of prey
grow old in their "isms"
shriveled up raisins
lifted from the ground
a pregnant rat
tries to catch the boat
upstream by entering
a bale of cotton
no one lynches him
Klansman grow weary
in their plight
their wives washing laundry
and cleaning sheets
attending meetings
and January "White Sheet Sales"
at the Penny Store
in Philadelphia
a small vulture
searches for
diminishing

returns
an alone barefoot black girl
sits on the edge of a
pine log
looking downward
humming sometimes
"It 'Causes me to wonder
where has the grim
reaper gone
and when will
the grim reaper
return?"

Boats unloading
berries
boats unloading
berries
slaves
being led
blindly
from Africa
remains
gathered
and
buried

blindly

There exists no more
Natchez Indians
but there is a
highway named after them
and a town
in which they lock arms
sing
and walk into the river
until the tribe drowned
they heard about those
that were walked to death
moments before
on the trail of tears

Chains
clinging
change
chains
choking
choking
chains
change
only money
change
exact change
change
from reconstruction
to would be assailant

and back too
chains
borne by slaves on ankles
slaves
lurking
with chains
lurking about
chains
borne by innocent prisoners
open sores
and a gathering of blisters
chains
of Parchman prisoners
a black man's history
chains
the American past
present
and shame
and chains
if chains
could be
change
broken chains
but still chains
exist

It was one winter during the 40's when
Vettis called out, "Doevail, Doevail! I got 'em, I

got 'em!" I was sitting in the out house trying to relieve myself but by the sound of her voice, I hurried, wiping my rear end with corn shucks and running out.

I looked at something I had never seen before - Vettis holding Little Junior with his pants down and his face wearing embarrassment, with a tapeworm on its way out. So I hollered out to Vettis, "Hold him, and I'll get a stick." "Hurry, I can't hold him much longer," she replied. I looked at the muddy ground and remembered that mama had given Little Junior some homemade medicine just yesterday. I picked up two sticks, hurried over to Vettis and continued the operation, forcing the tapeworm out. Ten years later, Vettis recalled the operation of the tapeworm, never letting Little Junior outlive the event.

Words like injustice
having no meaning
to vultures
they linger blindly
with nothing else to do
but justice is blind

and scales
never really ever balance
humidity and the smell
of cheap beer
on the vultures' breath
they carry out tasks
the surgeons general
out in the woods
flocking and dancing
around their burnings
when will they ever
learn?
blind to the despair and poverty
they created
truth
shattered
flood waters raging
graveyards under water
caskets afloat
afloat
vultures at prey
though already
dead
interpreted
as justice

And on Monday
it's out to the woods
to chop wood

to heat the kettle
to wash the clothes
Jerothea's got a strong back
And makes love like a woman
she uproots trees
wrestles cows from
the pasture
and cooks with a passion for Leoz
when sickness comes
but Jerothea
makes love like a woman
she chops cotton
chops weeds
chops off the heads
of snakes
and makes love like a woman
Jerothea
moans
and moans
and whines
and come morning
it's back out
to the field
to bail hay
slop hogs
and fry fish
everyone knows her
as Jerothea

and she makes love like a woman
and in the evening
it's pots and pans
and boiling greens
okra
pepper
and the mess
skillets gone
with grease flying
Leoz knows her as
Jerothea
and Jerothea makes love like a woman
she can shuck corn
pour White Lightnin' on a scar
shuck and jive that man
and make love like a woman

Henry Mack
stood bent over
hacking away at some
pulp wood logs
in preparation to load them
on the truck

        A voice came from out of the woods,
"Henry, Henry!" and one of the Jackson Brothers
answered, "We're over here." Henry Mack
stopped what he was doing and turned as Neicee

came through the wooded area short of breath,
"Alex Lee had to take ya mama to the hospital."
"What fur?" "She burned her foot real bad."

It was so late that evening and not enough
gas to make it to Meridian that Henry Mack
decided to go the next day.

Cora laid there on the second floor of
Mattie Hearst Hospital, moaning every so often,
and turning from side to side.

A few hours later, a middle-aged white
Woman came to dress the amputated leg as Cora
continued to moan and groan with more sorrow
in her moans.

Henry Mack got up so early that morning but
had to deliver another load of pulp wood in order
to get money for gas to make it to Meridian
and back.

That next morning Henry Mack pulled out
for Meridian in his uncle's car.

It was as if the middle-aged nurse slept
with the sound of Cora moaning even though five miles from
Mattie Hearst and returned to the sound of Cora
moaning the next morning.

A couple of hours passed and Cora's
moans grew painful coming from down the
hallway and ringing in the ear of the nurse.

Henry Mack was about another forty-five
minutes away, when the nurse decided she
couldn't take it no more, leaving the nurse's
station going into the room where Cora lay and
grabbing a pillow from the next bed, standing
above Cora for a moment then placing it over
her face and climbing atop the bed to place her
weight to hold Cora and the pillow in place.

Henry Mack arrived on the second floor
only to see his dead mother.

Another rainy day and another funeral,
and it was at the funeral that word got around
that Henry Mack's mother had been murdered.

Henry Mack cut pulp wood all that
summer, and as summer left so did Henry Mack
for Chicago, promising never to return.

Ruts
in the road
paths
to follow
in the muddy
red clay dirt
life
in ruts
and least one steers
away or off
these paths

from Toomsuba to Carthage
a muddy road
with ruts
and ruts
atop ruts
  here is where slaves
once walked in
formation
or offshoots of
ruts
slaves stomping feet
life pounding
like hoofs pounding
African slaves
Almost people
slaves in chains
with feet
  pounding
the midnight sun
goes underneath
dry up ruts
and burn backs of slaves
hot steel
melted
and years later
after the burning of Freedmen's Bureaus
even into the 20's

A black man

ridden by fear
his wife's shame in her womb
icy roads
and worn ruts
but send the daughter away to Memphis
to abort the baby
icy roads from Toomsuba to Carthage
the midnight moon
and a frozen snake
crossing the road
in the distance
slaves can be heard
feet pound
as one wiggles in death
and disjoins her child
words travel
like African drums
back in Toomsuba
a mother cries of her shame
troubled in her womb
her husband comforts her because of creamy blackman
but the petty bourgeoisie
continues on
in ruts

The north wind blows
an angry wind
scattered from above

skimming across
the river
the river is deep
wide in crossing
the river is deep
long in crossing
the north wind
blows
the rain comes
in a fury
a mule seeks shelter
left out in the rain
pebbles become
blood waters
the wind grows
and blows
the river widens
death can't even cross
but somehow
a rat
survives
working hand in hand
with burning crosses
a black boy
is bitten by a rat
a preacher stands in fear
the river is deep
long in crossing

let us not grow weary
as to seeing
the coming of
the other side

Freedom cries like a lonely ring in a bell,
coming from a distant place. Mr. Rogers pulls in
from the rain-soaked highway in his new 1943
Ford. A beautifully wrapped box under his arm;
he hurries into the house and out of the rain.
The ride from Jackson was long and quiet.
Lengthy, especially when one is alone and
promises of joy await the opening of the box.

Mr. Rogers dries off the best he can,
walking out his back door with the box in his
hand.

Sadie already heard him pull in moments
ago, greets him at her door with the rain and
troubled waters.

The two children have been fed lunch, and
Sadie had just finished churning butter although
Mr. Rogers would have bought butter for her had
he known.

He pulls the dress out of the box after
holding her in his arms for a moment; her face
becomes joyful, though pressed. But the dress is
beautiful, and he holds it up to her and he too is
pleased. The two children stand in the distance

between the doorway, looking on waiting to be
summoned by both mother and father.

A fish pond
dried up
though once stagnant
Negro women
dressed as domestic workers
riding in the back seat of their
employer's automobile
infiltrated wombs and violated standards
bear children
with bleeding blisters
showing
a rip torn mulatto
standing
in a muddy roadway passing
but that's the way of
life
and that's the way of a
soul to bear
for who are children to
question what love is made of
let alone
what love is based on
although some children
have so much love
and ponds dry up

and justice
becomes stagnant
and love diminishes
leaving a soul to bear
mulatto of the south!
Mulatto of the south!
The prelude
And the interlude
once called
nigger
the anger
a lone hand points towards
a vulture gnawing on
raisins and gifts in the
middle of a dried-up pond
ignorance
becoming healthy

No voices
no faces
no words spoken
everybody's granddad
had a mule named Doc
and he could poot silent night
but the children worked
harder than the mule
and now
they work their children

sorry is
a sorry word
the culture of poverty
is a sorry place
but racism bears

a scar to wear
so send the
jack-ass
to Jackson
dammit just
get the jack-ass out of this
house
so off to Jackson
to the insane asylum
see ''Cause
the world
ain't right!
naw it ain't right!
see ''Cause
racism is a
heavy scar to bear
like that
red dusty dirt
it gets into
everything
and everywhere

see ``Cause
see ``Cause
mama beat me
and I left alone

cross the bridge
over the swamp
before day
see ``Cause...
see ``Cause....
see ``Cause.....

thoughts of trains
with hands grasping
rails
trains
of thoughts
hands
reading out
with picks and shovels
laying blacktop
laying trees
lay tracks
for trains
black men's faces
missing
mothers
and signs of

"colored people only"
where people went
all aboard!
All aboard!
train leaving
fine job for a
Negro these days
Sleepy-car Pullman waiter
nevertheless
it's still trains
and tracks
and trouble in my soul
trains of thoughts
deep rooted thoughts
and trouble up north
you know
Chicago
and no use going there
this summer
Rock Island Line
and auntie's biscuits
boxcar blues
with uncle Lee's pistol
one more train
one less gang
one more train
move on

cold is the night
warm is the liquor
but Mississippi was born
with the rain and the fury of
the red dust
warm as the summer's morning
but hard is the death
tracks
and trains
transporting caskets
and more trains
of thoughts
passing

A Dixie flag hanging over the edge of the
front entrance of a gas station. Almost out of
gas, Gully pulled in for service, but before he
could stop his motor, a bullet rang out and
through his wind shield. Quickly shifting
gears and speeding into the roadway, Gully
didn't have to look back; he heard a voice
deliver words of "Nigger, get out of my gas
station!" Another shot rang out, barely missing
Gully's skull this time, coming through the
bottom edge of the window. After a hard day's
work in the Delta loading cotton bales in the
warm humidity of the evening mixed with the
pines and magnolias adjacent the road would

provide a tranquil ride home or Gully thought it would.

Lawd done delivered again. Still the anger boiled up in Gully and about a half mile down the road he got out of the truck, knowing he wasn't followed, but knowing he was almost killed.

"Ya prejudiced bastard."

Pause
moments await time
history awaits occurrences
revenge
more sheets
equals more revenge
and no one can stop
revenge
children at play
waiting for events
children beget children in the
red dusty dirt
mixed with humidity
and revenge
and souls press other souls
and perhaps
children from long ago
await revenge
no justice here in this

statement
but truth is seen
through the spilling of the
red dusty dirt to ashes
that is
plagued
with revenge
two lovers stand
trying to forget
about tarnished sheets
stand atop the pine needles
that wore holes in the road
and before that the ruts
both lovers wonder what would their
love be like
conflict certainly does
play a part
once again the sound of a
mockingbird can be heard
and a woodpecker runs down
a barbed wire fence
Mississippi was born
and with meaning
but not meant in
a hollow log
but just rot away
time standing still
lovers gather

trying to make babies
Sunday dinner wanting to be free
others hiding
aside a hollow log
who knows?
maybe waiting for time to rot away
machines pull cotton off that rusty
barbed-wire fence
and a Whoo channey bird
continues to fly north
trying to outrun its
shadow
another quiet cow pasture
where men and women gather
pine needles
a mockingbird couldn't
determine whether they
were lovers or not
struggling through the remains
of red dusty dirt in a hollow log

IS, THE COLOR OF MISSISSIPPI MUD

It was so hot, until amidst the sunset, you could see
humidity before it fell upon the gum trees. Even the
ticks and chiggers lay under maple leaves left
behind from the autumn prior. Heat hot or
forever sweating, it didn't matter, Mister
Hoffstein had another hundred acres of former
timberland to be converted to pastureland and
another hundred acres of hay to be harvested.
So for Sandy Martin and O'Dell Jr., they had
enough work to last the entire summer and it

figured that if they worked hard as planned, they just knew they'd be coming back for autumn and next summer too.

Planting, tilling, plowing, and chopping, there was a week more for baling hay, on Mister Hoffstein's place. Sandy sat drivin' the beat-up truck and O'Dell Jr. throwin' or should I say pitchin' them bales. I mean pitchin', 'Cause he musta weighed a good two fifty and stood a little over six feet. So strong he was, that he could lift one bale with one hand and chunk another with the other hand.

The lonely sound of a robin came from deep in the woods about two hundred mess of 'em. They stumbled down the muddy road with the mud thick on their heels, passing the bottle every so often. "You could get in the ring with him, O'Dell."

"Like shit, Sandy!" "You can get in the ring with him."

"I wouldn't stand a chance. But O'Dell, you'd kick dat nigger's ass."

"Sandy!", O'Dell said, like a backwoods preacher, "I could drink all dis bottle and a few moe, and you still couldn't get me in the ring with Joe Louis." "Yes sir!" Sandy replied raising his hand, "'Cause he's ah knockout

fighter." "Yes sir!"

"That's right!"

A whoo channey bird stood quiet in the middle

of the road. Feet were moving in

the distance, but neither one noticed. The sun

falling and creating dust. "'Cause he's ah knock

out! Fighter!" "Now gimmie dat bottle!" Just

before O'Dell could hand it to him he heard the

sound of a shotgun being cocked, and made

ready to fire.

"Yall just hold it! Rite dare! And get cha hands

raised high." It was the Sheriff from Toomsuba

and his partner, and they caught both O'Dell

Junior and Sandy Martin with an illegal bottle of
liquor in a dry state.

Bootleggin!

"You wanna tell us where you got dis liquor?"
But, O'Dell said nothing. "You don't know
nuttin! Huh nigger?" "You don't even know you
a nigger!"

Still O"Dell sat still, looking straight into their
faces and not answering. "Go on, lock em up
Barnett. They ain't gonna say who did what
or who got what." So they took them to jail
cells, locking up O'Dell first and then Sandy, but
they put the guns away for the moment. The
Sheriff wanted to question Sandy, about <u>his</u>

curiosity. Now Sandy Thom Martin was real

fair skinned, with wavy hair almost straight.

Matter fact, he could at certain times and for the

fun of it go into the restroom assigned for

whites only. So Sheriff Perkins and Barnett

came into the cell and told Sandy to get up!

Sandy rose while O'Dell sat up on the cot and

 turned to look from his cell. "Now, I ben trying

to fur out, something. 'Cause you is out wit that

dare nigger! And you out drinkin' moonshine.

Together. Now, ain't dat right?" O'Dell Jr.

caught the sound of the question and felt

something was wrong. He stood up and came

close to the bars as Sandy tried to be polite and
answer, "Yes sir!"

"Now you don't look like no nigger. Or not to
me! But me and my partner Barnett been
talkin. And he says you's a nigger!" "I tol em
You's a white man!"

Why O'Dell Jr. knew Sandy like a brother, and
even better than a brother. He knew how Sandy
wouldn't back down and even though he looked
white, he would never allow himself to be
counted as a white man. Sandy leaned forward,
looking straight into the face of the Sheriff and

with a cutting grinding voice, that drowned out

the sound of O'Dells' yell of "Sandy!,Sandy!"

he answered "I's a Niggah!" and quick, like

the dropping of a bale of hay onto the fluttering

feathers of a robin, came a pounding fist against

his back and a punch to his stomach. Sandy rose

just as quick as he buckled under, and plastered

a left uppercut against the chin of the Sheriff that

sent him falling backwards against the bars.

Then turned to go toe-to-toe with Barnett,

exchanging fist for fist. But O'Dell knowing

otherwise began kicking the gate as hard as he

could yelling; "Come on! God help me! You

can't leave hi 'em with them ober dare. They'll kill 'em."

Barnett and Sandy threw punches for over two minutes. Then the Sheriff got up and rubbed his chin, looked over at O'Dell kicking the bars and said, "Niggah you ain't going nowhere!"

"You sonna bitch! Open dis cell." "Come here and fight me. You

peckawood!" He yelled trying to provoke him any way he could. But, the Sheriff knew who O'Dell was and feared him, knowing he could take on two of them easily. So he swung and hit Sandy on the side of the face at the same time that Barnett caught him in the nose with a hard right. Sandy stumbled, only to fall into an oncoming punch by Barnett. "Yeah, you's a nigger." the Sheriff said and pounded Sandy in the face and in the stomach while Barnett held him.

O'Dell calling out, "Sandy, Sandy!" Continuing to violently shake bars and to kick the cell gate trying to break free as the gate rattled and Sandy fell to the floor. And that's when the two of them began kicking him until blood poured out of his mouth and nose.

O'Dell called on God, hoping for something or someway, he could get out and fight them but now there was blood all over the floor.

The Sheriff delivered the last blows, kicking him in his

privates and leaving him on the floor
unconscious.

They slammed the bars shut, then walked to
where O'Dell stood. O'Dell backed away hoping
they would come in but it was as if they set out
to break his spirit, saying to him, "Ya friend's on
the floor, nigger." Then he walked out closing the
entrance door.

O'Dell gripped the bars and shook them for a
moment, called out, "Sandy!"

There was no answer. Again he called out,
"Sandy!" No answer. O'Dell slid down to the
floor shaking within himself, calling out, "God!
and then Sandy. Awe naw." Writhing and

weeping with a loud "Awe naw, naw God!

"Aaaawe!" For there was still nothing he could

do.

IS THE COLOR OF MISSISSIPPI, MUD
Section 2
IF THE NORTH COMES, MOVEMENT

Hollering misty
        Come stiff
                Come hard
                        Or maybe an angry fist
        I tells you that north wind
                Ah is strong wind
It pulls the river upstream
        Like a mighty wind
It blows the limbs of trees
        North it blows
                North it blows
Buckling knees
        It holes
                Shakes
                        Stirs up the blues
                                Stirs up the soul
That north wind blows
        A mighty wind
I tells ya so
        I tells ya so
It could be time to run again

        In the wind or next door
Fate

        Could catch us
All of us
Time to run again
        With us
Before
        There is none of us

        A spoon-shaped fork in the road, 2 roads
crossing close to the Delta. Humid air hanging
around, clinging to moss. Two cars, older
models, travelin' down the highway headed for
Al-J Section of New Orleans.
"Honnee, I'm gon' meet ah dem 7 sisters, and
have 'em tell me everythin' bout my future, foe
it comes ta pass," I said.
Vales shrugging her shoulders, and pulling her blouse near the top
button, in an attempt to gain a coolin' of air
about her dusty brown breast. Her arm hung out
the window. Her hair was plaited in tight braids,
and sweat was fallin' from her face from the
Delta humidity. She wasn't really even listenin'
to anythin' that was spoken. The dust litin'
against her skin bearing a song to her worry.
        A path of dust rose from the ground goin'
upward into the air, as the gray Ford continued
down the dusty highway. Eltee, pressin' his foot

against the gas pedal, and every so often
listenin' to Alex talk about meeting the 7 sisters,
combined with the music of Ellington's "Take the
A train." Vales was still a long ways from
Harlem. Battlin' with the thought of never
seein' Harlem or any other part of New York.

The sweat on the palms of Henerie's hand,
became as cool as the dust that seeped into the
car every so often. Why worry, he thought to
himself, maybe it could work. After other folks
went to Al-J for different kinds of problems,
they was cured. So maybe it could work, but
what if it don't work? The thoughts of Vales,
were goin' in the same direction, as the two rode on
tormentin' themselves by listening to the words
of the others in the car. Their words became
distorted as they headed for New Orleans, and
their hopes bent on a secret voodoo cure for
Syphilis. Again Alex spoke, without receivin'
much of an audience. "You, dey say, them
peoples over in Al-J can do a whole lotta strange
thangs."
Silence still remained within the car,
along with the dust and humid air.

Get up, mule!
    Get on up, mule!
I say, "Get on up from dare
    Ya lame-duck jackass!"

The moon sat still last night
While dis ole mule
      Sang and poot
      Sang and poot
You wanna go north too, mule!
      Dat why you sing and poot
           SHIT
I'd leave yor hairy ass
      If I could
      Go up north dis evenin'
          Or right now
      If I could go up north
I's ah tellin' ya and you sing and poot
      Ya ole sorry jackass
I'd go north and
          Sing and poot

Cities

McComb	Cannon
Greenwood	Canton
Collinsville	Louisville
Biloxi	Pocahontas
Gulfport	Vicksburg

Fleas, ticks, and high waters
Drownin' the presence of the future
Why not?
      What not?

And not a wade over, mirror-hung
Dirt-filled chest-a-drawers
        Left sittin' in the rain
Makes ya wonder
More Tabasco sauce please
Country
        City
                Country
I am gonna up and leave here
        Misbelievin'
        I gonna leave
You hear me?
Wit you misbelievin' self…
But the rain falls and
        The varnish deteriorated
Off the red clay dirt
        Of an antique chest-a-drawers
Stay behind child,
        Stay behind
Winter is cold
        Crops need tendin' to
Room for one more
        Friday evenin' fish fry
Just too much racism comin'
        From outta the clouds
And prejudice is a filthy word
Monday mornin'
Came Monday

You's still here
        You's still here
More tabasco sauce please
Leavin' behind prejudice statements
Cornfields, pastureland,
And angry tabasco sauce
All for a ticket up north
Train station at Jackson bees crowded
1936 is a very good year
for plantin'
it's an even better year for leavin'

memories
looking at a pullman porter
not havin' ever been exposed to anythin'
        past the Mason-Dixon Line and a cotton field
somebody's train is bound for glory
Chicago or Detroit
        I just can't make up my mind
A brother and a sister in Chicago
two first cousins and a sister in Detroit
the steam pumps outward
        from the locomotive
carryin' a stench in the air
        headed straight up north

                    greetin' a new found racist
indignation shockin'
                         simply shockin'
No use tryin'
        no use cryin'
                sun done pass
                        moon done pass
                                tears ah cryin'
early mornin' dew drops conjure up against
        the settling dusty dirt
one rusty plow stands
        in an unplowed field
that once gave birth to
        sugar cane, corn, cotton and the like
all dem Browns, Jacksons. Smiths, and the
like
done left
        behind
a lone mule
hawlin on wheat grass
        under a tree drippin' sap
bustin' up the dirt
memories of his master
drivin' him up the hill
        and through the pepper patch
hummin' and wishin' and makin' the blues
how he too could have gone north

        2 deaths back

        represented 3 years
1 flood
        was 4 years havin' passed
2 children born
        represented 5 years
3 deaths
        represented 2 years
the hot summer
        represented 6 years passin'
the birth and death combined
        was 1 year
a year with good crops
        represented 1 year, 1 marriage, 1 birth
and 1 long hard winter
        represented 2 years in passin'
1 death represented 7 years since the passin' of
time
related to events and time passin', relative to
people's lives.

Breckenridge man
        I's yor boy
Yor boy I is
Breckenridge man
        Gone on wit the wind and foe
                Why don't cha cry some moe
        Breckenridge man
                You've torn hearts
                        Into rusty ashes

                    Floatin' downstream
Coverin' the river's edges
Hail, Mississippi!
         Hail, Breckenridge man!
                    Hail, Mississippi home!
Sorry longs to the lonely man
A heart of hatred, Breckenridge man
         I's ah goin' home
                    Heavy trees moan
                           The dead you know of groans
Babies whimperin' in the mud
                           Whimper on,
Breckenridge man is gone
Like other shadows and would-be memories
         Uprooted from the shores
Pass away, stolen souls,
         Pass away.
                    Hatred gone home,
         Movin' with the river
         Downstream
                    Downstream
         River deep
                    River deep
         The funnel is long
         The funeral is wasted
         Breckenridge man done gone
         The river pulls us north
         Downstream is the pull
         Quickenin' are the chains

Forgotten bees the history
Memories are the pain
River deep
River wide
Sorrow hour owls cries
The river pulls us north
Go north, young man,
                Go north!
The north star
The northern lights
And down home the river pulls us north
Warm is the soul in making
Weary are the nights
In the end the grasping of another hand to
Live
Down home
Ohh sweet bird
        Past evil
I see thou flies north
Downstream goes the river
The river pulls us north
Armpits at the day,s end
        Carry songs of sweat and toil
            About to leave
                        Leave
Gasping breath
        Speak to the moon glow
            Flee

Flee
Weary hands up from the mud
Tell of the north hoped of
        North
Late at night the river
Pulls us north

        North
One more day
One more sun
        In passing
One more son
        In passing
Remember death, it costs so much to bury a son
these days
All payments due in poverty
One more day
        One more cornfield
                Mistaken
For a greener pasture
One more day
One more sermon
        To bear
Best to leave McComb
While things pass away
The rhythm of the rain
                Bearing
One more day
        To bear

Cry me a river
Sing me a river
Turn the hand of time around
    Face
River
    Face
        Face the river
Up river's edge
Shadows creeping on time
With midnight
Lips
    Flee
The river whispers
Face
Swift is the river's edge
Sharp is the rivers
    Face
Shadows tip past the evergreen moss
Bearing gifts of pain
    Hidden faces borrowing the river
        For exploitation
Face cries the river
The river drowns
    Faces
Face the river

"Hey boy, you wanna pop,
    you wanna pop?"
sittin' still underneath a rusty red-painted

Coca-Cola sign
"Come get ah pop boy."
Daddy gone north, and mama is out plowin'
Church tonight
All ah McComb ah be out tonight
And some folks think
Ah pop will getcha salvation
But up north will leave ya
When the chips is down
Done played out
Mud is here
Laughter
Done played
Might as well go to church
Ain't nuttin' ta do on a Sunday night no way
Maybe Friday payin'
But not Saturday
Loose leaves
Falling
        Hurry come autumn
Sing Reb
Sing
The folks at church is killin' too
Just like before
Wishin' ya had ah pop
But not really wantin' one
It's the time that passes by
        And by

"You wanna pop, boy,
          You wanna pop?"

Socialism, uncanny stench
          Thoughts about leavin'
Colonialism, Democratic stash split, filth
Evening mist rising from the setting sun
Like mildew hang around
          The pond
The South is placed highly
Throw out Intellectual Ideas
Well over
Train
Train
Boat
Boat
There's room for more discussion
                              Well
                                        Well
Communism, sharecroppin', boll weavil, cotton
bail

Train leaves Jackson at 3 o'clock

Same ole stuff
          Stand in a stagnat pond
Whisperin'
Home
          And releases me
                    'Cause

'Cause
Last night the cow gave birth
It made sense
The bull was bored
            At last the answer comes
            Because I run

The storm cometh
from the south
                movin' north
carrying strong turbulent winds
        entered the Gulf Port at 2 o'clock
carry winds at 12 o'clock high
Fright,
        The night may not see morning
And no sun in sight
Hurricane, storm, tornados, floods
Natural disasters create a phenomenon
Of sudden social cohesion
And time and time again
Flood, hurricane, tornados
Whites-only sign
        Afloat in 4 feet of water
Winds so strong, it ripped the colored
                Waiting room
Moved it to the white section
People care

And unexpected klansmen were saved from
drowning
      By a Negro sharecropper
          Unknowing
Just giving
      In a time of need the whole damn house
          Ripped apart
Now bearing whites that say
             Pray for me
A Cotton Mouth wriggles out of a tree stump
After the storm
And in search of prey
The people drawn close, move apart,
To abide in a racist state

Showing no sorrow
      About the storm's destruction
Before and after
It remains
Not even watered down
It remains
Colored here
      White only

Damn near got that right
      Wasted piece ah sweat
          Cries lips "Sing"
             And free me

Yes, Lawd!
Free me too!
Tears, promises, be fallen
More tears from down on the farm
And dammit
Whatcha marry me for?
The blues of you
The blues of myself
Tomorrow's sorrow and yesterday's memory
Sing poverty songs to whisperin' crowds
Of chain gang workers hoping to link up
north
Lips cry, eyes see the further beyond
Hand of love stressed beyond measure
Eyes peak out, whispering to the world
Hold me, love me
Hold me
'Cause I am here down on the farm
Lips sing in the spirit of a dance
Sing
And lips in da mood for love
Sing baby, sing!
Melody
Sing for me, lover!
Melody
Sing
The mule done gone
The cow done left too
And arms cry hold me

                    Love me
                    Hold me
         Don't ever turn me loose
         Oh yes, oh yes, the mule done gone
                    The cow left too
         You tell' em
         Yeh they is gone
                    'Cause I set 'em free
         16 days toward summer
         and a woman wants more time than a man can give

              Sunday evenin's goin's on near Mount
         Salem again. The people in the community were
         tryin' hard to hold onto their neighborly quality.
         It seemed to be leavin' fast. The conquest to
         leave and go north sorta created a pressure on,
         and for those left behind. A dilemma of whether
         to humble and bear it, or refuse and leave. Some of the
         choice surrounded new shoes.
              Leathee looked over her shoulder, while
         standin' at the picnic table, to have her plate
         helped with a piece of ham. She caught the gaze
         of brown eyes lookin' at her.
              "Sho lookin' nice today, Miz Smif," he
         said. "I see's you should know, Willie Alfred,"
         she told him, "after all, you been lookin' me
         over from head to toe." In which he returned,

"Why, Miz Smif, I am sorry, but I just couldn't help but look at cha."

"Why, you can call me Leathee," she said. "Why you must not mind me lookin' after all." Willie told her. "Why, Willie Alfred, I happen to notice your new shoes, myself." She answered. The two helped their plates get full, and found a wash pot, and a choppin' log to sit on, only a few feet away from the congregation. "Well, Willie, ain't cha gonna tell me where yah got dem shoes?" she asked questioningly. "Oh yeah. my brother up in Chicago sent 'em to me," he replied. "Is you goin' north too?" she questioned even more. "Ah ain't rightly sho. I'm thinkin' bout stayin' here, and startin' my own woodcuttin' bidness," he answered her. "I thought about goin' north myself," she told him. "Besides, my mom needs help farmin.'" "Well, Leathee, if they laugh at chew, its 'Cause you's a pretty woman," Willie told her. "You think so?" she asked, slawin' on a piece of buttered pound cake. "I know so!" he returned. "Oh yeah, how you know?" she continued to question. Catchin' himself with a glass of lemonade to clear his throat he said, "Why it'd take a long time to tell ya." She told him, "Go ahead."

They married that day at church, and lived
through the death of their first baby, the death of
her mother, the death of their crops, the lynchin'
of their neighbors.
The misery of livin.'
　　　And the beauty of love.
They never did go north,

　　　　　And never could.

　　　They got the dogs out
I ain't done no crime
They got the dogs out
　　　I won't do no time
Don't wanna do no time
I gonna leave 'em behind
They got the dogs out
The big bloodhounds out
They won't smell me nowheres about
They got the dogs out

There was being spreaded on the top of an ole
shack
The humidity of summer heat
As chains grew louder in the distance
Gospel songs were bein' sung
Deep
　　　Deep
　　　　　River
Days have passed since the nightriders were seen
Ghosts in a Ford automobile

Now in its rhythm
The gospel songs carry a warnin'
And in the distance
      In the distance
Chains can be heard
Gospel songs can be heard
The remembrance of war
Carryin' a host of people
    Tryin' to get away
Burning and burning
     And in the distance
       Chains can be heard
Chains that drag the river
The fear of faces
    In the distance
       Gospel songs bein' sung
        River
         Deep
          River deep

Be bop
    Be bop
Shew due, be do
And all fall down
In the middle of autumn
Right here wit more red clay dusty dirt
You've gotta get a grip on yuself
Boy I tells ya
You gotta git a rite

Says the real right Reverend
And so bees the culture
      Said the preacher
More be bop
      And more be bop
And more work needed for the lonely
sharecropper
16 notes that decided time and fate
16, 16th notes that were never played
at anyones funeral
we bop ah lee bop
      we bop ah lee bop
16 notes and 5 pages of unwritten words
      that confessed the blues
      and Madison Avenue got the shit confused
a lone voice cries
      I ain't been here before
The culture baby
      The culture
The moss hung from the trees
The neighbors hung from the trees
        They cried
    Be bop
    Be bop
Was so busy tendin' to the share-croppin'
      Until the culture cried
We bop
      We bop was busy tryin' to get up north

Until the culture cried shame
Just plow the field, Walter Lee.
     Just plow the field
More work needed to produce rhythm for
Madison Avenue

MISSISSIPPI

The moss hung from the trees
The neighbors hung from the trees
They cried

Be bop
Be bop
Was so busy tendin' to the share croppin'
Until the culture cried shame
Just plow the field, Walter Lee,
Just plow the field.

More work needed to produce rhythm for
Madison Avenue
The bigots played on it
And the state justified it.
So the culture sought refuge.
Sing the blues for me, Lola.
Sing, baby,
To the sound of drums and chains.
Will the culture keep the culture.

16-16th notes tryin' to beat out shame
Rhythm and drums that beat out chains

We bop ah lee bop
We bop ah lee bop
De bop
Never again
And never again

Carthage
The sound bores a tremble
Within ones soul.
Carthage
Again the Spirit shakes

A lone bird
Once dancing on an electric wire
Crosses the borderline.
Carthage
Ropes and chains
Whips and flames.
Carthage in history.
The word comes slowly Dragged from in
between
The tobacco-stained
Teeth of middle ageless
Right man
Carthage spittin' hatred into the mud
White lightnin' to soothe the memory murder in the midst of
Every letter is sounded
With meaning and fright
Carthage
With barbed wire dragged through her throat
Run, Billie, run
Past tar, past feathers
And into the mud of Carthage.
Like loving arms
Cotton falls from trees
The sound of its name
Rotted-out hands, ghost-like and muffling screams
The cotton falls to the
Ground and into the mud.
For the rope is decaying because of too much blood?
On this tree in Carthage
That once bore bitter fruit.
Swaying
But the sound strikes again, Carthage
Mourn the death you bring
So many times over
Day ole auto grease beer and cheap
Wine
For the right white sheets

Hands clenched too
The evidence destroyed
Like Billie's voice ravaged by
Time and scars
Carthage, Carthage.
A sorrowful blues
Is pounded from out of a church
House door in Carthage.
No doubt while right folks look.
The blood-stained mud
Bearing rain and dust in
Carthage.

Carthage
Cotton falls from its trees
Like the sound of its name
Rotted out
The cotton falls to the
Ground and into the mud
For the rope is decaying
On this tree in Carthage
That once bore a strange fruit
But the sound strikes again, Carthage
Like Billie's voice ravaged by
Time and scars
Carthage, Carthage
A sorrowful blues
Is pounded from out of a church
House door in Carthage
No doubt while right folks look
          The blood-stained mud
Bearing rain and dust in
Carthage

End of the day
      For Thursday
Rush us Friday
And pound the drum-beats
inside heads.
Step light over muddy puddles
With this casket
Prayin' and asking God
Why me, Oh Lawd, I didn't
Want her to go.
A soft pat on the back can
Ease this pain
Like poe folks always do.
3 o'clock in the middle of
The cemetery
Satisfaction hopes to bring
Their loved one back.

Across the muddy puddles
      Distant swamps
      And tears that fall like rain.

Sing it sister,
Tears that fall just like rain.
A wasp's nest
Near a hog's pen

Kinda stinging, I'd say

No meat
      To eat
And no slop to give.

Say you better
Slop dem hogs

Maybe a snake will come
To eat the wasp and be fed.

Feed for one lonely hog
Looking forward to some
Hoghead cheese.
And the children
Why day up der in Chicago.
They can't eat that stuff!
Wit collard greens in the
Front yard packed in
Like animals
Having run away.
And Mississippi does miss them
Wee and Me.
   And eye
Sits around hummin'
Bee boop
   Beep beeps
To an invented tune
Somewhat dilapidated in
   Thought
But just enough
To pass the time away
   Away
     Away
      Away
With dilapidated buildings
   And scared walls
Facing scarred people
   Inside
   Beats of be boop
     And wee
Now my time has run out
   Done gone past the last half note

No moonshine
No thoughts of inspiration
Hope sat on a toadstool

And what the shit done gone.

One more day
And one less dollar
And moe life
And one less mule to
Listen and holler
One o'clock
Clock train
One more track
One more day I am Chicago Bound
One day I can't say
That I'll be back.

Ropes
        And lies
                In a fool's paradise.
We all go fishin' round
Covered up roses tarnished with stains
More ropes
        Breaking justices
                In justice
Endless ropes
        Instead of hooks
And chains
Hooks
        And chains
Justice
And ropes
Tarnished stains
        remain
                remain
In remains
Of hooks
        And chains
Wrought just again
Ropes and lies
        And hooks and chains

I am gone to upward bound, on a train or a boat, on to Blue
Island, Williams Street or Hell's Kitchen. It'll be a blessing
if I don't make it no further than Beale Street. Joisey packed
for Finnly a half a pan of cornbread with a jar of buttermilk,
which she placed in a croaker sack for his lunch. Finnly was
mopping up the last of molasses with a biscuit.
    "You best hurry," Joisey told him, standing at the back
door.
    "I gets paid today," he told her, rising from the table,
"so I'll pick up some cod liver oil for Albert Junior."
Finnly gave her a quick hug and headed down the road for about
three miles to the lumber yard near Meridian.
    He was stacking wood as usual, and anything else that
Mister Pitworth desired him to do. Mister Hopkins also gave
orders sometimes to Finnly whenever he desired, using the term
nigger. Finnly was working alone. The two Freeman sons were
about a hundred yards away operating the saw. Finnly took it
upon his own to place the four-by-fours on the flatbed. He
was working so hard that he didn't notice the sound of Mister
Hopkins coming up behind him. The forward motion of Finnly's
body sent him towards the train car. He tried to catch himself
in between a stumble, but one hand caught the edge of some four-
by-fours, and about three came down on him. "Shit," Finnly
said, as he fell to the ground with the four-by-fours.
    "You cussing at me nigger? No one told you to stack those
posts to that train car." Finnly was trying to get up, with anger
that cancelled the feeling of pain 'Caused by the falling
four-by-fours.
    "Ya trying to move before your time, nigger."
Finnly didn't even look at Hopkins, he just threw a six by six
towards him with his fist. But Hopkins had fallen
onto the edge of a brick, against his temple, and was dead.
Quicker than lightning, he picked the body up and loaded it on
to the train car, stacking four-by-fours around and on top of
it. One track over sat the one o'clock freight, headed
to Tennessee. Finnly rolled the cart to the warehouse, picked
up his lunch of cornbread and buttermilk, walked back out
towards the trains, waited to see if anyone was looking and got on the
one o'clock train

One more day
And one less dollar
One moe life
And one less mule to
Listen and holler
One o'clock train
One more track

One moe day I am Chicago bound
      Bound
One day I can't say
      That I'll be back

Itta Bena
    Is where the sand struggles
Against dusty clay red dirt
    Until the Mud turns to a Silky Soot
And when that evening sun goes down
    You can see that mud shining
Like Satin Brown
    And underneath that Satin Brown
Washed by the River's Edge
    Lie the bones and lies the blood

Hail, Mississippi!
    Deep river in crossing
Hail!
    Mighty is the river
Sorrowful is the blood
    Long is the day that never ends
And how just is the mud?
    Having covered these Delta graves
That only a simmering blues can soothe

You ever see a man crying to his death
    Filled with his own blood
In the middle of a red clay dusty road
    Or ever see an old woman, dressed in poverty,
Clinging to pain?
    Until justice decayed the skin of her bones.
You ever witnessed suffering
    Running upstream
Crushing hope and long, long-awaited dreams
    Hail, Mississippi!
Hail!

My soul has seen enough.

Bitterness so strong
It could hand-pick bales and bales of cotton
Anger so refined
It plowed acres upon acres of mud.
That reddish clay
Dusty dirt turned muddy
By Blues
By mercy
And by the blues of river's edge
Coming forth to hail you on.
As in Hail, Mississippi!
No Hail, Mary!
Oh no!
No Hail Mary's!
For not even Mary could imagine
Mud mixed with blood so strong
Not even blue steel could plow up
Merciful ends
So hail, river!
Hail on!
To rage on,
And wash the muddy blood
Through our veins
And come by night
Midnight if you must
Like night riders,
But don't touch me.

And don't taunt me or threaten me.
For I left Mississippi with tears
And time enough to see a man
Become nothing but blood turned death,
Turned over into that mud.

Twenty-five years later, Albert Jr. had become a minister,
and went to visit a cousin in Chicago, but not even a cousin
knew where Finnly was, or who he was. "Why, you awfully young
to be a minister," Sister Hattie Pearlie Jenkins remarked.
"You must have studied from your father,"

"No ma'am, my father left Mississippi when I was three."
knowing all along who he was, she asked again, "Well, what prompted
you to be a preacher?"
He looked straight at her, then towards the ground,
answering, "It just seemed like one day that Jesus put me in a
place of being at love and charity with my neighbor."

She then took him for a ride in her new Cadillac to 42nd
and State Streets where a man was selling peanuts. She
parked and told Albert Junior to get out.

"You eat peanuts?" She asked him. "Why sure," he had a
puzzled expression on his face. She pulled some money out of
her purse, and gave a whistle. Then yelled, "Hootubee!" A man
came from the middle of the street with a box of peanuts.

"How you, Hootubee, how you?"
"Fine myself." Handing her the peanuts and taking the money.
The traffic and noise of passing cars was loud.

Hootubee asked, "Who's this fine young man you got wit
ya?"

"It's you son."
And looking at Albert Jr. she said, "He's your father."

MISSISSIPPI, DON'T YOU DO ME WRONG

Poverty, oh poverty and prejudice
Across my hand
Mississippi don't you do me wrong
For I was raised from
This mud
This soggy reddish mud
And all my life
It's been tears
Atop fears
I ain't seen nothin, nothin but blood
My neighbors
They all sing about being carried home
And it's been sung
For so long
Until it
Sounds like the blues
The blues
Running through
My veins
Poverty, oh poverty
And prejudice across my hand
Mississippi don't cha do me wrong
Poverty, oh poverty
When will I ever see
Tranquility

FAITH DRIVEN BY THE REDDISH MUD

What makes a human being different,
From a bird in flight,
A colorful butterfly,
Or a cloud that changes shape in the sky?

 Mississippi as a distant cry
From the fantasy Golden Dream of California
Mississippi was born of the red, clay, dusty, dirt.

So when cotton was high and time for pickin' come near,
She was busy shootin' a pistol with one hand, drinking
corn liquor with the other and buck dancin' to a
12 bar blues of Ma Rainey
Bessie Smith And John Lee Hooker

Mississippi has been a teacher to us all.
As daddy sat on the front porch tellin' stories about
The eyes of the <u>Griot.</u>

And years later, Miss Gert continued this fine ole family tradition
in the essence of the clay, red, dirt that surrounded the ole schoolhouse
where she broke switches off trees.

To press for the high more of Negro excellence
And years later they still calls her "Miss Gert, the School Teacher"
Why Miss Gert says, "I seen sorrow and sadness in my life time take me to
where there's joy and laughter". We can sing about Jesus and all the
troubles we seen, but tell me what makes a human being different from a
Bird in flight,
        a colorful butterfly
                or a cloud that changes shape in the sky?
Only God knows why we are the way we are
But tell me what moves a human being
                        To change this Red Clay, dusty dirt.

Lou Next Door

Louisiana Prisoner Ended

I wonder who you are
In this one more day
We spare ourselves
Confinement hour
Love is, a stranger to who I am
A strange
Mercy misguided
And not to be found/near
Evidence: Jesus
Plea the 2nd person
On the cross
Behind him, not a show of us
Him real in body and flesh
This is all I have
And still, I am not him
Death row/cage; chair, cared for
Locked to the institution/table
Needles pour forth
In his arms, to shutdown life
Death
I feel it could have easily been me
Executed daily
Instead of him
Born poor

Longley dead drunks, tarnished by
Pain and plight
Having raised hell to affect that

Which was left
Now we embrace ourselves in murky waters not noticing the nightingale's
Deceit of the blind woman calling
Leaving through the dark
Dredge the rivers bottom and search
For ravaged souls
Surrounded by a dream of never-ending pursuits
Kinky intercourse; in fancy dining hall
Limousine service to the orgy, and
Trading of existence
And now we know it all; having bore
Witness to the possessed passion
Roaming within a fleeting moment of
Greed and power contrived
A split second of peace cause's the
Mind to wander through swamp waters
And a canary to flee its limb
If it had not been for the gospel
Preached on Saturday
Sorrow would have needed a place to
Live alone
Now in the quiet, a sparrow picking
Bones of matter
Everyone seeking their own, as I
Join their happy journey
Slipped into the deranged to make
Hell, home
Whispering to the misty wind to spare me,
For I know them not
Once warned, not to go near, nor
Even follow the frolic
In a soup bowl full of voodoo
This jungle of altered states,
A prophet's message discarded, now
Feared

Nebulous mind bending, spellbinding
Forms of evil be seated,
The fun filled voyage has brought
Us here
Where satan awaits
And the hallway night light
Reflects the exit sign
Reading there is no escape

Brimstone waters spill over our
Thirst
Only to quench the nightingales'
Calling
For the less hidden desires which
Pain our
Flesh and lust, in between greed
And wealth
Wrapped in sovereignty of self and
A state of mourning
For the apparent selfishness
A caricature
Painted in a grinning disguise of
Paisley blues, Monroe to Shreveport
Humming in between gospel songs
Running owl of madness, and pain
The tongue;
So hard to speak
And like prisoners unchained; we
Kill in an effort t to ascribe to
Thwarted hate smeared by an obscure
Artist too drunk to wear his
Disorientated mask
Rehabilitate ourselves
Of fate and realism
Angola, whisper to me, Angola
Lying from coffins captivity
"No! Not me." Whimpers the voice of
The innocent
A raven nearby; plucking out an eye
Placed there to sit to still

As his hand maiden extracts the
Gold
And this is where we all have come
To
From each and every tooth
Having arrived on hot ice and well groomed turpentine
Here at the crack of
Dawn
And bearing witness to a rotting
Truth before then

Next Case/Step Right Here

For sale to peonage your way home
Justice truly blind
To the touch of silver
Like the statue
She stands, near sliding snake
Eyes hypnotic
To the Coptic
A captivating glare
Snake sliding up the stairs
Over taken justice
Gold and stars fall from her scales
We.
We weep
Shy beg for mercy with snake venom?
We can't go without tar and pitch
In her thigh, still alive
We/
We the people
Bury her
And wait for another

Soul Inside the Minstrel, Me, Man

Nether hear our humble cries and
Pity not
The caged bird that roams around
Behind bars
And pity not I, neither when I die
To your shame.
Couple your hand near the
Reflecting pond,
Past rocks and down gravel roads
Callused hands and hearts spread
Before your dancing spats.
With hands near the pond and holding
No disguise
Pity not the babies waving good-byes.
Gaining no answers to all the
Questions why, yourself, writes to answer home
Your smile, your sorrow was all a
Masquerade in disguise
The minstrel man,
Oh yes! The minstrel man, bird free
Then out of his happy rage
Gathered the bird in flight
To be;
Imprisonment
Both singing to a life of misery.
With the bars surrounding his

Painted face and chocking grin.
Like those who chain gang works
Pounding, beating and bleeding for
The minstrel man, with hidden face
Worked hard to hide his sacred
Sorrow
In serenade of bluesless blues,
Oh dance; oh prance and dance.
The cake walk, the peg leg and
Buck dance;
With black face, painted white lips
Oh minstrel man, pity not the shame
We bare
Crushed like rock, to gravel and
Gravel to sand.
The minstrel man, would smile
With a relentless pursuit to endure
His own hurting song. Smile; a
Mile wide smile, not knowing from
Whence we came, his history or his
Name;
Like many other folks tossed to and
Fro,
He didn't even know who he was
The minstrel man; oh yes!
The minstrel man sang a sane song
Of liberty to set the caged bird free.

The gandy dancers lay the tracks
That lead upward to the sky. Past
Clouds and hills of rain soaked
Sugar cane,
While the chain gang workers
Muffled their cries and covered
Their sighs.
Pounding rocks for pain
Each thrust of the hammer is
Different,
Yet it's all the same
But the minstrel man yes! The

Minstrel man was already dead, to
His pain, dead to his flesh and
Dead to his bones.
And me wondering when will
I ever leave here

The Plum That Left On a Blink

Rapidly running roses
Cross Canal street
In search of switch blade, trimmings
And day ole pussy
Dice flowing out of briefcase like
Blood
Spilled onto a blond wig resembling grass,
Here were slaves once danced throughout
The dark
Painted by the will
Well running water
And the hook
Driving that bass home
Like a diesel across the highway
Here we are bumpin'
To the muddy swampy song "Oh Baby Aw Baby!"
Hang out to dry lullaby
Monday wash sheets, T-shirts
Funky drawers with blues to match
Mosquito gravy going home to that place
Of blood stained hands share in a quiver
Singing to political men
Of many faces and favors
A begging song for life
Chump change spread-eagled
Similar to 30 pieces of gold spread out
Three card spread over
Trinkets and spells to fight back
When the deal is cut
Through the torn flesh, sizzling
Hot money
Over pussy

Music is everywhere, snap your
Finger
In flavor pursuit
For a cohesive body
As the hooker says, "I love you"
Why the horse drawn carriage rounds
French quarter at 2:30 in the morning?
Body parts in plastic
New Orleans cooking spices of rosemary to cover the
Scent
Board the ferry to AL-J last stop
A prostitute lost
In New Orleans fog
In search of a pearl
Five fifty for a taxi to the French quarter
5 o'clock trash pickup
Gumbo dumped
The music ceases to be echoed
Over the red light refusing to blink
Which one do you prefer

Swamp waters gleaming as never before
In mid day moonlight
Oily and smelly
To the stench of
Blind man breathing
Swamps fragrance
Like music it's everywhere
Swamp waters smelly to the touch
Day ole hard rock candy disguise
Narcotics floating on a tub/like waterlily blooming
Bones, blood and dust lie beneath
Inseparable to the
Stench of swamp waters

Hound dog barkin' "Go Back Home"
Angola Penitentiary ain't no wheres
I belong.
You know where there's swamps
There's oil and where there's oil

There's money
And where there's money
There's corruption,
And where there's corruption,
There's death
Cause the wages of sin is death,
Smell it lingering.

Shreves-port or Shereveport
Why don't cha give up livin'
And move to New Orleans
Monroe!
Why don't cha just grunt, hush, and moan
Tululla! Tululla!
Don't call me no more.

I was down in New Orleans
I was down in New Orleans

O Mister Warden
O Mister Warden

Why do you treat me so mean
I was on the corner when
A gambler up and died
And I don't know why I cried
I tell you yea, I don't know why I cried
All I know, I was on the corner
Just about to find my way
I was down in New Orleans
I was down in New Orleans
I told the judge

I waddn't drunk outa my head

I saw the gun smokin'
I saw the gun smokin'
And the gambler had a hole in his head

Down in New Orleans

Down in New Orleans

I told the judge I waddn't drunk
Outa my head
But if you kill me too
I for sho'
I'll be dead.
Down in New Orleans
Down in New Orleans

Imprisoned by Denial Then Touched Free

Storm wheel roller
Rolling down cobble stone streets
Chasing ghostly face of fete
Pass up the wheelchair victim/begging
Sink to the cash
Cabbage/greens packed by success
Mildewed dollars stink.
Here we dodge thee noble hound dogs
Running through knee high weeds
In search of nostalgia
To create the upchuck
And dressed in heat hot fury
Greased dollars turned over back alley deal
Ones, become buttered down empathy
We scream "it's 5 o'clock!"
Some nuns in transplant uncover their intentions
For the sake of sport
Spoke softly "now give us beer,
Freely."
Here out west the wheelchair
Victims
Run for their lives

With kangaroos eating their hot
Dogs
To elements in absolute proportion
To one another, ice and electricity
We turn cornbread over in the pot
With black-eyed peas
And ask one of the sexy nuns "This
A hit,
So let me roll on it."
Liberty in sorrow
And wealthy enough to impress a
Deaf mute
"Roll wit me baby" she told him in
Sign
The blind man with a red suit on,
Is actually her honey
All the way from California to
Bogalusa
She pulled her tit out
On the grey hound
"Touch," she whispered
So he would know she was for
Real
It's better than rejection, being
Horny and
Living on the edge of dusk.
Canceled like a stamp dried and shipped
Out; anyway
Last call for alcohol; 1:45 A.M.
Lights are all blinking
She is trying desperately to admit
Being something other than an
Effect of the cause, (being an event
Which pushed her towards the
Monastery)
He blind and touching
And she being a nun, has left her convent
Lonely feeling desperately to
Forget Mary and feel.

A shotgun house
A lantern held high
And it's not a train yard
With a light swinging
Or to give
Signals
Couldn't let Louisiana satisfy
Swamps run alone
So this drifter, staggered in
From Mississippi bitter cane
On the run
From sun 1930's farm band
He owed a lot
Hot money
Not land
But nothing but his park street
Wheel driver
Run amuck
With casket on a bar and gun in hand
Discourageable /bounty due
Blaze the smoke
Left behind by lantern's swung
Signaling "Move on in for the kill"
This time it ain't nigger
Or po' white trash on the run.
So much moisture in the air until
The fast pace of his run
Creates a dust that turns muddy
To the rivers tongue
We hunt coons with this light
Stronger than lantern
More insightful than a bolt of electric
Hounds closing in
Train wheels approaching
Dark fog surround all the moss on trees
Guns drawn about to bloom and become
Smoke
Sweat bellowing
A drop off the muddy ledge
Train wheels roll over a grunt

A head chopped off
A frogs eye motioning
The big farm bounty hunters
A job well done
Gun smoke clears
A path in the fog
Train whistle blows
Over –Marengo-swamp

Sing oh church, sing
Underneath the cotton dust
On rivers bottom
Lies the tracks of my misery
Sing gospel songs, sing
Shriveled up buds headed down
Stream
Pain soaked, over laid down with
Varnish- stain
Sunk deep into my skin
Pine wood turpentine bleeding to the color of this box
Now faded and everlasting
Sing gospel songs, sing
Near to the cross
The tracks of my tears
It's where the grease and gravy is
Served
Sing church house sing of me

Foot-feet-steppin' rhythm
Running perpendicular to the mid
Set
Of the 2nd line
To give us all a feel for what
Death is for
"Oh, prance and cake walk
You know who I am"
So weak it comes to home, in the form
Of numbers to gamble and wrote on a
Napkin
It's not me!

"So work harder," calls a voice
Ghostly from the past.
From the shore lines
Of a deathly groan
Step lightly and grind harder
This time it's the paid for
Prostitute,
In red lace and pink
Was last seen combing her hairs on
Charles street
Breathe the filth of someone's
Unclaimed salvation
Here a grunt/is needed
Valentine savoir pray and pick your melody
Lone string on guitar, while
Bleeding heart
Sings/and it sounds like
Ocean-sprayed cat fish
From up here on the roof
With a breeze a windy cry gone hush
Perhaps? We can all go sailing by
And pray.
For the sweat on the poor man's face
Feels like another crusty piece of poverty
Dilapidated hot humidity
To me, it's all the evidence I need
Cause misery to dry up/ my tears to pray about
That light that always moves
Swaying from one of the ceiling to the window
Tell me, is Tennessee Williams on
The city bus with the broken
Headlight, winking
At the crescent moon?
Somebody ought to fix that thang!
Leaving Canal Street abandoned; can
Be so disenchanting
The full moon does not claim residence
Anywhere near here
It sits out back
Where the colored folk once used to

Be served
Hell! They didn't complain, why
Should you?
An ex-priest finger fondling the way
Vagina of a fresh hooker, in blue
Bra and purple panties
Even though it looks like catsup on
The cats eye/saved
Here on the toilet seat they act
Out love,
Lovers, kissing, lightning bugs conger gating
Love
Or just a thrill fuck
She moans and he prays, for her to
Devour him by reason of insanity
This was a trick.
Me baby!
Whisked away, a speeding four door
Her daddy driving Chevy
A siren talking; one flashlight;
Numbers 4-68
Played straight
No lighthouse to cover the shore
Light slinging water front or harbor, just
Light from a match-ticking.
Now the presence of a cop, sniffing throwing
His weight around the corner
Screw us all over
Time and time again
Cigar being chewed on, nervous twitch
Finger, and crusty humidity
"Oh, Mister Poe-lice man
Shake; shake em on down.
Plight stops flashing in the
Loading zone
Maybe, oh yes!
Pussy could have been for free!
Pass Bourbons Street lingering
The whoo doo is coined as a phrase
To create a party

Spread dust into the magical air
It's a bluff
In the fun, in the frolic, with the
Gun for fun
New Orleans roulette similar to Russian roulette
Musta been some skin diver, pulling
Dust
From rivers bottom
To ease your misery in the taboo
Being born to remember ashes
The memory of Anthony James
Gone
Lost rites, Lost supper, Lost shit
Lost smile
Hole in the arm
Patch work-needle work
Hole in one
Hole in the man/man's soul
Hole in the nude dancer, swinging
Back and forth
Hole life in the pound cake, along side
The green Jell-o
Discovered, after his execution
Out of the darkness of the night,
A drunk man sole
Revival; down Tulane and turn left
At the 4th light
He was actually telling the truth
When he was drunk enough
For Jesus! To fight corruption.
Can I get a whiteness to the
Manwhole cover up
Being born by the river – deep
So soothing, to hum, moan, and sing
About
So easy to sway along side the melancholy
A grazed catfish sees a body
Floating
Fat dollars in hand
Clutched

Payment past due
Held tight as a rosary
This is where most of us
Tarry and cry our way home
Sniff, pork fried turnips, boiled okra too
But a rivers bottom, tomorrow
Arrives on satin sheets
And shakes, snakes, and jagged
Glass
So he is served shark stew
And you thought it was beer. Chopped hops
Broiled – steak
In shark stew at $24.65 a plate
And up from the gulf
The nightingale has spoken
Dinner being served, once it's not
Political enough
Chill first then dish up
A full order of barracuda
while on
Board the cruise 9:00 straight up,
At night, and hey! You got a nickel
For the slot machine,
An old woman in white, with long
Ghost white hair, and long ago,
White dress, dragging the cobble
Stones
Her hair is corn braided, handling
Snuff
Yells to blind man tapping
"Ain't cha got nobody to hap ya outta here!
You out and ain't even got no cup.
You needs to ben some home, cause
Lawd ye ain't gots no money."
Gasp one more cry, before we make
It home
Before the cotton washes ashore
Bloody gospel
11:30 the second prostitute screams
To her poe pimp

"If only you would have been here to hap me."

We fought back, continuously
In the forties, in the fifties, in
The 60's
In the shame of it all
And the colored people especially
Now weeping for themselves around
Congo square
Where slaves once stood to fight
Back/on the auction block
And now the city streets, such a tragedy
Even the cobble stones
Bulging out from this murky waters
Touch fog that sits oily and
Greased
Sink almost into death
Libo Lebo limbs begging for life
This almost tree
Leap frog with bubble eyes
Resembling almost tree
Bulging belly bottom of algae
Round hoof of ghost wind sighing
Slow phase
Speaking in the macumba
Instead of the simple Algers voodoo
A tree like an escaped slave
All the way from Brazil
Running to the dance of the most
High
Can double back
Through the swamp
Mingle/Oh no! Stranded in Louisiana
Boney bottom
Without deaths departures bearing
No limbs,
Now in – a state of limbo
Pray he may find home
Having once fought for life
Sweet magnolia tree

Speaks/even in the ghostly song
Murmuring "Oh how I need thee."
Caring a Brazilian melody of murky
Shallow swamp waters song bluesy to soothe

Next Case/Step Right Here

Justice truly blind
To the touch of silver
Like the statue
She stand whimpering, near sliding snake
Eyes hypnotic
To the Coptic
A captivating glare
Snake sliding up the stairs
Over taken justice
Gold and stars fall from her
Scales
Which fall for her eyes
We.
We weep
Why beg for mercy with snake
Venom?
In her thigh, still alive
We/
We the people
Bury her
And wait for another

When sleep don't come

In the present
Moving force of spirit
Mind causing lips
To sink
Speak why am I here
An ageless question
An ageless question

At 2 in the morning
An atheist
In the presence of soul bearing
Thoughts
Causing insides
To shiver, be shaken

And sit still
I, we, all of us in the presence of
God
Feeling like dirt being moved
Being carried home
I trust

Correntha had niece
Named Malenthia
Sure, surely sure as
Molasses dragging of buttermilk bottom
Of Malenthia's mildewed stomach
Where, where
Much of Louisanna had inhabited
Sittin', sitting up
Staring the dishwater
She used to cook wit
To make
Leadbelly soup soggum'
Pie on jellyrolled okra
Thighs on that pea hull
Mattress, where she would
Sang, "Lover man
Oh lover man, I gotta go, I gotta go
Away from who you are."
Nothing but a meal left
Behind her infatuated
Intestines, and crying out
At the third hour
For God, country
And conversation to comfort
A memory imbedded like
The day
The county man
Came to drag Hammonds
Swamp
Hammonds swamp for
Another ravaged body
Hammonds swamp where
Malenthia played

At the age of seven
Come eleven

No less
No less desirable
Now
As she was then
To middle aged men
Who sat
Who sat on the plywood porch
Sitting and waiting
Sitting and waiting
For Malenthia's mother
To hurry
To hurry up and finish
And as the sun
Would fall over the tops
The tops of pine trees
They would feast their
Hands upon Malenthia's
Thighs
And wait
Wait for her
To make that gurgling sound

Roaches
Roaches would crawl
From underneath the
Front door/ yellow jackets
Yellow jackets flew
From out of the slits
In the screen
But Malenthia's mother
Would hide her screams
With a chicken feathered
Pillow held tight
To her embrace
Somewhere past
Louisiana dusty roads

And shriveled up
Shriveled up
Cane fields
And years of weighted
Down urban living
Up north
Found the two women
Malenthia and her
Mother
Enchanting the face
To face encounter
With the God of
I am, I am

In a spiritual yearning
Burning
To feel their unbridled misery
And so deeply sat
That mildewed carpet
In the middle of the room the
Room the stench
The stench of it
Running over
And over
Like that picture show
At that one
Movie house back home
Running over and over
The thought
Finding the two women
Once again
Murmuring to themselves
In regard to the spirit soul cry
That beckoned the
God shaped space
Within
From deep within
The two women
Murmuring back

"We gotta go
We gotta go
Away from who
We are."

Jives Blues in New Orleans

Jive was to be
Smooth, blended in with
Quarter note
Overlapping to become
The ferver of the
Jodie grind. Not the
Ace boon coon but kinda
A little bit of the
Harlem shuffle
See, Jive was the
Essence of the musical
Beat in between the
Language of bop and
Bop city
As to become
Hip and blend in with
The Negro mood. Cause
That's how we felt
And only we could
Interpet it in c minor
Or A flat. The rhythm
Was contained in the era
And jive was the expression
Of the Negro turned
Into the black asthetic
To cool down the anger
Of Central Ward with
Cops running for their lives
Of C. L. Franklin's church
Blasted by armed gestapos
Only to have the Republic of
New Africa leave court
With clenched fist
Jive was the mellow part
Of the melody asking to be
Left alone after another
Set back and discourage men
Dampered its soul upon

Returning from Vietnam
But now Jive has become
Watered down. See cause
Jive knew what existed
But dropped the anger of
His history now after witnessing
The thousands of floating
Bodies Jive knows it must
Never trust the smiles of
Klansmen in the Whitehouse.